Out of This World

A Christian's Guide to Growth and Purpose

By David J. Swandt

Out of This World: A Christian's Guide to Growth and
Purpose / David J. Swandt

Published in the United States of America
ISBN-13: 978-1497460775
ISBN-10: 1497460778

For inquiries about this book, please contact us by email at
ootw.dswandt@gmail.com

With special thanks and gratitude to Shoreline Church in Austin, TX:

Sr. Pastors Rob and Laura Koke

Pastors Sam and Kelly Mata

All of the staff and volunteers of who helped touch many lives through the Out of This World ministry

To my entire family for their continuous love and support

Out of This World
A Christian's Guide to Growth and Purpose

Table of Contents

INTRODUCTION

The very beginnings of this book originated half-way around the world a number of years ago during a short term mission trip somewhere in a remote region of Botswana, Africa. It was over several campfire discussions that a great friend of mine, Pastor Sam Mata, raised the idea of developing a ministry at our church focused on engaging and helping new and recently re-dedicated Christians understand their new-found faith in clear and simple terms, and provide them the foundations needed for a lifetime of growth and purpose-filled living.

Our church, Shoreline Church, is a thriving congregation of more than 6,000 in Austin, Texas. Shoreline has a special emphasis on welcoming people of all ages and backgrounds into their fellowship and into a strong and vibrant relationship with Christ. It seemed to be a perfect setting for God to do something wonderful and meet a real need.

In the coming months and with the help of countless staff and volunteers, we launched a pilot of "Out of This World" – a Christian foundations training and outreach ministry using draft materials and a basic framework for the class as a starting point. Over the course of the next 18 months, we experimented with different approaches, solicited an enormous amount of feedback, observed what worked well, and also what didn't, and finally assembled all of our learnings into this book, "Out of This World: A Christian's Guide to Growth and Purpose".

In the following years, we have had more than 1,000 people attend the program at Shoreline, and have had other churches, home-group Bible studies and ministries employ the materials as well. It has been an honor to see how God has used this to build and strengthen so many.

While I could go on, let me conclude by thanking you for reading the book. If you're a new or recently re-dedicated Christian, you'll find this to be a great foundation to build upon in your walk with God for the rest of your life. If you're more seasoned in your faith, you'll not only find this to be a great refresher, but also an excellent approach to help frame a clear and simple way to communicate your Christian faith to others who may inquire.

Either way, I hope you enjoy it, and are encouraged to grow in your walk with God.

Sincerely,

David Swandt

June 19, 2013

Chapter One

THE BIGGEST DECISION OF YOUR LIFE

INTRODUCTION: Should God Let You Into Heaven?

Just imagine for a moment that your time here on this earth had come to an unexpected conclusion. With overwhelming wonder, you find yourself standing before your Creator. As your confusion and awe turn to anticipation and excitement to finally see your eternal home, you are suddenly stopped before entering. God asks you a penetrating question, "Why should I let you into heaven?"

How would you respond?

Thankfully, when that great and wonderful day arrives for each of us, God will not ask us to complete a test prior to entry. Nevertheless, the scenario paints an important, thought-provoking picture intended to help us better understand salvation.

Some may respond to God's question by referencing the good things they've done. Others would describe their faithful church attendance, and still others might list all of the bad things in life they've avoided. While these are important elements of every Christian's life, they do not guarantee salvation. There is only one correct answer to the question: *I have made Jesus Christ the Lord of my life, and He has cleansed me of all of my sins.*

God Created us with Eternity in Mind

When God created us, He had much more than a 70 or 80 year plan for our existence. He has a specific purpose for each of our lives. His plan spans both our earthly life, and our heavenly (or eternal) one. James 4:14 describes the difference between these two aspects of our existence. It says,

> *What is your (earthly) life? It is a mist that appears for a moment and then vanishes.*
> *James 4:14*

You've heard the saying, "Life is short." In light of eternity, it is! The Bible says,

> *...man is destined to die once, and after that to face the judgment. Hebrews 9:27*

All of us are subject to a physical death. But physical death is only the termination of our physical body, not our soul. Our soul, or our conscious existence living inside our body, is eternal. Our soul will spend all of eternity in one of two places after our physical death: Heaven or Hell.

Heaven is eternal paradise where God lives.
Hell is complete separation from God.

Our natural birth into this world was not only the beginning to our temporary, physical life on earth, but also our spiritual life here and beyond through all of eternity. So in light of eternity, some may see our earthly life as insignificant, but this simply is not true. Your eternal destiny is actually determined

10

by the decisions you make during your time here on earth; most importantly, the decision to make Jesus Christ the Lord of your life. Salvation is available for all of us through Jesus Christ, and through Him alone can we change our destiny from spending eternity separated from God, to spending eternity with God in Heaven.

"I am the way and the truth and the life. No one comes to the Father except through me." John 14:6

The decisions we make in our earthly lives are important for other reasons, too. The way we live as believers can have an effect on the eternal destiny of others who do not yet know Jesus Christ as their Savior. Every day, those around us are watching our example of living for Christ. As Christians, God uses each of us to bring heaven to those around us who do not yet know Him. Jesus said:

"You are the light of the world...let your light shine before men, that they may see your good deeds and praise your Father in heaven." Matthew 5:14-16

We All Need a Savior

When God created Adam and Eve, He made them without sin and in perfect relationship with Him. When they disobeyed God's command in chapter three of Genesis, they brought sin into their lives, and also to the entire human race. Romans 3:23 describes the far-reaching impact of Adam and Eve's decision.

... for all have sinned, and fallen short of the
glory of God. Romans 3:23

No one is exempt from sin and its effect; every one of us is
guilty. As a result, we are all separated from God. Our sin
also results in an eternal consequence.

For the wages of sin is death. Romans 6:23a

Because of Adam and Eve's decision to disobey God, death
became inescapable for them and all of their descendants (the
human race); both physically and spiritually. After their
failure, God was faced with a decision: to allow sin to run its
course with mankind, resulting in the extinction of the human
race, or to provide a means to save mankind from sin's grasp.
Thankfully, as the ultimate expression of His love and grace,
God provided a means of salvation through His Son.

"For God so loved the world, that he gave
his one and only Son, that whoever believes
in him shall not perish but have eternal
life." John 3:16

...the gift of God is eternal life through Jesus
Christ our Lord. Romans 6:23b

Apart from Jesus Christ, mankind is destined for both
physical and spiritual death; there are no exceptions. But for
those of us who are in Christ, physical death still awaits us,
but spiritual death (Hell) does not. Rather, eternal life in
Heaven awaits us after we leave this earth. Through the
perfect sacrifice of Jesus Christ and His resurrection from the
dead, we escape the spiritual penalty of sin!

Salvation: God's Part and Your Part

Your salvation brings together two important decisions. The first decision is the one God made long ago to send His Son into the world to be our one and only Savior. The second is your decision to receive His Son as YOUR Savior.

For it is by grace you have been saved through faith and not of yourselves, it is the gift of God - not by works, so that no one can boast. Ephesians 2:8-9

GRACE is defined as unmerited or unearned favor. Grace is God's part in salvation, and He extends His favor to mankind in the form of the perfect gift, Jesus Christ. Through the cross, Jesus made the full payment for the penalty of our sins. And through Jesus, the personified grace of God, no amount of good works is required of us, or could ever be paid by us. We cannot earn our salvation; it is a free gift available to all, requiring no payment on our part.

FAITH is defined as evidence that something exists even though it cannot be physically seen or touched. Faith is needed for our part in salvation, and by faith, as an act of our will, we choose to surrender our lives to God by making Jesus the Lord of our life. Having received by faith God's grace through Jesus Christ, you are undoubtedly, without question destined for an eternity with God in heaven. You can be 100% certain of that fact!

13

While good works cannot earn our salvation, they do play an important role in living out our Christian life after we've received Jesus.

For we are God's workmanship, created in Christ Jesus to do good works, which God prepared in advance for us to do."
Ephesians 2:10

God has a specific purpose for each of our lives, the details of which are largely between you and Him. But God has a common purpose for all of His children, and that is that we put our faith into action by doing good works. When we do, we fulfill an important part of God's plan for our lives, and we have the privilege of shining His love to others. Salvation is both a new beginning and an ending and is cause for celebration. You are a new creation, forever changed!

Water Baptism: A Public Declaration of a Changed Life!

Water baptism is an important way to publicly declare your salvation. Water baptism celebrates the ending of an old way of life and the beginning of a new one. Jesus taught the importance of water baptism to His disciples just prior to His ascension to heaven after the resurrection. He said,

"Therefore go and make disciples of all nations, baptizing them in the name of the Father, the Son and the Holy Spirit."
Matthew 28:19

Throughout the New Testament, there are countless stories of believers being baptized. Water baptism holds significant symbolism to both the one being baptized, and those observing. Water baptism publicly illustrates: the ending of your former way of life by being immersed down into the water; the beginning of your new life in Christ by coming out of the water cleansed, purified and a new creation in God.

Luke 3:3 represents water baptism as a "baptism of repentance," and emphasizes the importance of publicly declaring we've turned away from our old life and sin. While water baptism does not save us nor cover our sin, it does represent a critical part of our Christian life – a declaration that you're a new creation, a changed life! If ever there was someone who did not need to make this declaration, it was Jesus, who lived a sinless life here on earth. But Luke 3:21 says,

> *"When all the people were being baptized,*
> *Jesus was baptized too." Luke 3:21*

Jesus was baptized so that we would follow His example. The importance of water baptism cannot be overstated. If you have not yet been water baptized, you should consider making water baptism a priority. The Bible instructs us to make a public declaration of our salvation, and most Bible-believing churches provide many opportunities to get water baptized. Following Jesus' example is always a winning proposition. God will richly bless and reward you for your faithfulness and obedience to Him!

A Closing Consideration

If you have never received Jesus into your life, or if you did at one time, but are no longer living for Him, you can make a new commitment to Him TODAY by saying a simple prayer out of the sincerity of your heart. That prayer may be something like this,

> *Jesus, I know that I am a sinner, and only you can set me free from sin's penalty. I ask you to come into my life and cleanse me of all my sin. Help me to live for you in every area of my life, every day of my life. Thank you for coming into my life and setting me free!*

If you prayed that prayer with sincerity, believing Jesus will do what He said He will do, you have just received salvation, and have altered your eternal destiny to be with Him forever!

Chapter Two

GIVE GOD FIRST PLACE

INTRODUCTION: God's Place, My Prize!

First place - it is the focused ambition of all who compete. Whether an individual or team competition, the best score or time wins, and first place always brings the top prize to the one who achieves that privileged distinction. Always, that is, with one important exception.

Before our salvation, we usually hold first place in our own lives – living for ourselves, fulfilling our own selfish ambitions, promoting our own agenda. But when we become a Christian, first place is no longer our position to hold; it belongs to God.

Giving God first place in our lives began on the day of our salvation, but allowing God to remain first in all areas of our life is an ongoing process. When we do so, we live a fulfilled and blessed life in Christ here on earth, and inherit an eternal life of unspeakable blessings with God in Heaven forever.

Everyone who competes in the games goes into strict training. They do it to get a crown that will not last; but we do it to get a crown that will last forever. I Corinthians 9:25

God Has Given You First Place in His Heart

What would you think if someone told you that God sees you as if you have never sinned? The fact is, because of the redemptive work of Jesus on the cross, that is exactly how God sees you. As Christians, we are forgiven, cleansed and free!

That means you are a saint: one who has attained a special standing of righteousness in Christ. You are perfect, holy and blameless in God's eyes. He calls you His child, an heir to His abundance, and His friend.

But you are a chosen people, a royal
priesthood, a holy nation, a people
belonging to God, that you may declare the
praises of him who called you out of
darkness into his wonderful light. 1 Peter 2:9

Truly understanding how God sees us begins with how we see Him. God is not watching from a distance just waiting for us to make a mistake in order to punish us. Nothing could be further from the truth.

Consider what this verse says:

Yet to all who received him, to those who
believed in his name, he gave the right to
become the children of God - children born
not of natural descent, nor of human
decision or a husband's will, but born of
God. John 1:12-13

God sees each of us as His own precious child. He is a loving Father showering favor and care to us out of His endless compassion. Some scriptures in the Song of Solomon illustrate the incredible intensity of God's love for us by comparing it to the intimate love of a husband and wife. Hebrews 11:6 tells us that God is a rewarder of those who seek him.

God sees each of His children in a profoundly different way than most of us see ourselves. Understanding how God sees each one of us is founded upon the work that Christ began in our lives the moment we received salvation.

Therefore, if anyone is in Christ, he is a new creation; the old has gone, the new has come. II Corinthians 5:17

God made him who had no sin to be sin for us, so that in him we might become the righteousness of God. II Corinthians 5:21

This new creation is God's divine work; a complete transformation of our spiritual condition and inner person. He has completely forgiven and cleansed us from our sin - past, present and future. We are in right relationship with Him.

...as far as the east is from the west, so far has he removed our transgressions (sins) from us. Psalm 103: 12

We are God's people presented to Him without any blemish of sin; truly as His righteousness through the work that Jesus did on the cross. God has indeed given us first place in His heart!

God Wants First Place in Your Heart

In today's society, many base their worth upon wealth, how high they are on the "corporate ladder," how successful their business is, or even simply who they know.

But if our view of significance is established upon these things, we will only feel good about ourselves when we are flourishing in these areas. When our wealth and success diminish, our self-worth will also because our foundation is not solid. Jesus describes it this way:

> *"But the one who hears my words and does not put them into practice is like a man who built a house on the ground without a foundation. The moment the torrent struck that house, it collapsed and its destruction was complete." Luke 6:49*

Our identity is only as solid as the foundation we place it upon. By establishing our identity on the rock-solid foundation of Jesus Christ, our sense of fulfillment in life will not depend upon the changing condition of temporal things.

When Christ is our foundation, our stability is like this:

> *"He is like a man building a house, who dug down deep and laid the foundation on rock. When a flood came, the torrent struck that*

20

house but could not shake it, because it was
well built." Luke 6:48

Think for a moment of the many choices in life you may have to build your foundation of significance upon. These may include wealth, career, looks, family, fame, power or who you know. Are there others you can think of? Of all the things to establish our identity upon, only Jesus assures us of victorious Christian living.

But if you examine the other choices, none are bad or inherently evil. In fact, in many respects, they are very important areas of responsibility God has given us in our lives. But in the book of Matthew, Jesus helps us find balance.

"Therefore I tell you, do not worry about
your life, what you will eat or drink; or
about your body, what you will wear. Is not
life more important than food, and the body
more important than clothes? Look at the
birds of the air; they do not sow or reap or
store away in barns, and yet your heavenly
Father feeds them. Are you not much more
valuable than they?" Matthew 6:25-26

When we resolve this truth in our own lives, we find peace and fulfillment, free from worry and anxiety. This balance is achieved when we put Jesus first in all areas of our lives.

"But seek first his kingdom and his
righteousness, and all these things will be
given to you as well." Matthew 6:33

21

We all have dreams, goals and aspirations because God designed us to. But putting Jesus first should lead you to examine your priorities and motives as to why you aspire to do or attain the things you desire. When He is first in your dreams and aspirations, you're future will be filled with greatness and joy!

When God does bring a questionable motive to your attention, your most important response should be a willingness to make changes. Change can be difficult at times, but God always has our best in mind, and wants you to grow spiritually.

Winning Life's Battles with God's Help

There is a life-long battle that is being waged over our lives. On one side is the influence of that old sinful nature - those old lingering tendencies, temptations and sins that have been difficult for us to overcome. Over time as we mature in our walk with God, the influence of the sinful nature weakens. On the other side is the growing influence of the Holy Spirit's presence in our lives. These are two opposing forces as described in Galatians:

> *So I say, live by the Spirit, and you will not gratify the desires of the sinful nature. For the sinful nature desires what is contrary to the Spirit, and the Spirit what is contrary to the sinful nature. They are in conflict with each other, so that you do not do what you want. Galatians 5:16-17*

God's word encourages us to "live by the Spirit." In other words, we must allow the influence of the Holy Spirit to win over the influence of the sinful nature in our lives.

Many times, this is easier said than done. Our sinful nature prods us to make decisions to satisfy self-centered ambitions and passions. This is called temptation, and James describes it like this:

> *When tempted, no one should say, "God is tempting me." For God cannot be tempted by evil, nor does he tempt anyone; but each one is tempted when, by his own evil desire, he is dragged away and enticed. James 1:13-14*

Not until a decision on our part is made to give in to a temptation does it become sin.

> *Then, after desire has conceived, it gives birth to sin; and sin, when it is full grown, gives birth to death. James 1:15*

Amazingly however, as a part of God's profound love and grace extended to all Christians, God forgives us and cleanses us from all of our sins. We are absolutely 100% forgiven.

> *If we confess our sins, he is faithful and just to forgives us our sins and purify us from all unrighteousness. 1 John 1:9*

But there is still a danger in allowing sin to go unchecked. While God forgives us and cleanses us, He does not necessarily eliminate the destructive path of consequences and circumstances sin leaves behind. While God will always help us through difficult times, even when brought on by our own decisions, our best course of action is to do all we can to avoid making those decisions in the first place.

I Corinthians describes two important aspects in effectively dealing with temptation and sin:

> *No temptation has seized you except what is common to man. And God is faithful; he will not let you be tempted beyond what you can bear. But when you are tempted, he will also provide a way out so that you can stand up under it. I Corinthians 10:13*

First is that we're not alone in our struggle. You can know that there are other Christians, whether 30 days or 30 years into their walk with God, who still struggle with sin and temptation common to yours.

Second, is that God will not allow us to be tempted beyond a point where we're unable to make a decision to avoid sin. He will always provide a way of escape. Our job, as challenging as it may be, is to find that way out in the midst of our temptation.

The following section provides a Bible-based strategy for effectively dealing with sin and temptation. Putting this plan into action is one more way of giving God first place in your life!

Five Point Strategy for Victory

1. UNDERSTAND THAT GOD SEES YOU AS PERFECT, HOLY AND BLAMELESS, through the work of Jesus Christ. (Read II Corinthians 5:21.) Many times guilt and shame are the most destructive of sin's consequences. Understanding that there is no condemnation for those in Christ, regardless of the sin, is fundamental to victory (Romans 8:1).

2. CONFESS YOUR SINS. (Read I John 1:9.) Confessing our sin means acknowledging those sins first in our own hearts and minds, and then confessing them to God. Confessing our sin does not necessarily mean making them public to others. Confession is between you and God.

3. BE ACCOUNTABLE. (Read James 5:16.) Finding a close trusted Christian friend, pastor or family member in whom you can confide is an effective way to introduce accountability and prayer support into the battle.

4. AVOID THE SOURCES OF TEMPTATION. (Read James 1:13-15.) This is the most challenging point to implement, and requires some creative thought and planning. The truth is if you can avoid the temptation, you'll avoid the sin.

5. READ GOD'S WORD. (Read Psalm 119:11.) God's word tells us plainly that as we "hide it in our heart," it gives a special strength to say no to temptation and sin.

Chapter Three

INVEST GOD'S WORD INTO YOUR LIFE

INTRODUCTION: Guaranteed Returns!

In today's world, this statement raises some eyebrows, and also some suspicions. But there is a universal law that applies to nearly every aspect of life: the law of seed time and harvest, or put more simply, "you reap what you sow."

You cannot reap a harvest unless you've first planted the seeds. You cannot gain a return unless you first invest. You cannot receive the benefits of a product or service unless you first purchase it. You cannot retain physical health without a balanced diet and regular exercise. And with all of these examples, the return received is proportional to the quality or amount given up front.

The same law also applies to our relationship with God. We cannot reap a fulfilled and blessed walk with God unless we sow seed which will produce that harvest. The good news is that God has made good seed readily available to us - it's called His Word, the Bible. Sowing God's Word generously into our lives guarantees us a bountiful return on that investment.

Remember this: Whoever sows sparingly
will also reap sparingly, and whoever sows

generously will also reap generously. II
Corinthians 9:6

Overview of the Bible

The Bible is filled with timeless principles, clear instruction and relevant examples of living a balanced, fulfilled and blessed life as a Christian. In fact, God's Word never has, nor ever will become irrelevant, regardless of changing times and seasons, and is available to prepare and equip us to accomplish God's purpose for our lives.

All Scripture is God-breathed and is useful
for teaching, rebuking, correcting, and
training in righteousness, so that the man of
God may be thoroughly equipped for every
good work. II Timothy 3:16-17

The Bible can be thought of as an intimate written expression of God, and all that He represents to mankind. Below are some points to help define what this means:

1. The Bible is the tangible expression of an intangible God. It speaks of His attributes and character, His communication and commands, and ultimately His full expression of love for every person that has ever lived.

2. The Bible is God-breathed. While the 66 books of the Bible were physically written by many authors, each person was directly inspired by God through the Holy Spirit to write what they wrote.

3. The Bible is God's authority for our lives. Finally, because the Bible is God's "letters" to mankind, and the writings contained within are God-breathed, His Word carries the same authority over our lives as God Himself.

God's Word is one of the most important foundations of our spiritual growth and maturity in God. In order to fully allow the seeds of God's Word to flourish in our lives, we need to plant those seeds by reading it, developing our understanding of it, and then applying it to our lives.

Read God's Word Regularly

Most of us would agree that the Bible provides quite a lot of reading material - some of which may seem overwhelming and unclear at times. Here are a few facts about the Bible which will help you navigate through your reading time with a frame of reference and better understanding.

First, you'll find that the Bible is separated into two sections:

The Old Testament is a compilation of writings beginning with the creation of the world, the history of the people of Israel - including their defeat as a nation, the resulting captivity by their enemies, and ultimately their return to occupy Jerusalem once again a few hundred years prior to Christ's birth. The Old Testament is also God's law to the people of Israel.

The New Testament is a compilation of writings beginning just prior to the birth of Jesus, continuing with His life and ministry, His death and resurrection as our Savior, and ultimately the establishment and expansion of His Church throughout the world. The message of freedom in Christ by grace as revealed in the New Testament fulfills and replaces the need for the rituals imposed in the Old Testament.

Second, and generally speaking, there are three types of writings you'll find throughout the Old and New Testaments in the Bible:

Historical Account - writings which tell a true story and give an important historical perspective of people and important events.

Instructional Writings - books and verses which provide instruction on many aspects of Christian living, church organization and personal and family matters without specifically providing some historical account of events.

Inspirational Writings - poetic, artistic writing designed to encourage, uplift and express emotion from the author to the reader.

The New Testament writings which provide a Historical Account of the life and ministry of Jesus are Matthew, Mark, Luke and John. These four books are also referred to as the Gospels. The book of Acts is another historical book in the New Testament which chronicles the establishment and expansion of the Christian church after Jesus' death and resurrection.

The New Testament books which represent Instructional Writings are Romans through Jude. These are actual letters from church leaders giving advice and instruction to other Christians and churches throughout the world.

The Old Testament book of Psalms is a great example of Inspirational Writings. Below is an inspiration from a Psalm which assures us of the blessings God gives to the one who is investing God's Word into their life regularly.

But his delight is in the law of the Lord, and on his law he meditates day and night. He is like a tree planted by streams of water, which yields its fruit in season and whose leaf does not wither. Whatever he does prospers. Psalm 1:2-3

To plant the seed of God's Word into our lives, we need to make reading the Bible a part of our daily routine. As the seed of God's Word blossoms in your life, His blessings will become more evident. You will receive strength from His Word to sustain you, even through seasons of drought and difficulty.

If you've not yet made God's Word a part of your daily routine, start now. The New International Version is a great translation to begin with as it is written in modern English. Begin with the New Testament, and read regularly by giving whatever time and amount of reading you can joyfully give.

Do not be overly concerned with how much reading God wants from you each day. God does not have or keep quotas. Give of your time joyfully. At first, that may mean just a few scriptures or a chapter per day, but it's a great start.

Expand Your Knowledge of the Bible Over Time

Developing an understanding of God's Word is a lifelong endeavor. It won't just happen overnight. But there are certain approaches which can nurture a more comprehensive understanding. Here are a few thoughts:

1. Obtain some tools. There are several types of study aids available which can help you better understand what you're reading. For example, there are Study Bibles, concordances, and topical study guides.

2. Get involved in a Bible study team or small group to interact with other Christians and observe how others are applying God's Word to their lives.

3. Have a plan. For those who are really ambitious in their personal reading time, there are several one-, two- and three-year plans available to help guide you through the entire Bible. That's a noteworthy accomplishment to say the least!

The more you spend time in His Word, the better your understanding of it will become. As you do, you'll also find that God will help you comprehend exactly what you need to know for the season in life that you're in.

Apply God's Principles to Your Life Everyday

Your word is a lamp to my feet and a light
for my path. Psalm 119:105

For Christians, God's Word provides illuminating power in what at times can be a dark world. God's Word will only become that source of light if we are open to its truths and allow it to deeply penetrate our lives. Jesus describes this in a parable found in Matthew:

> *"A farmer went out to sow his seed. As he was scattering the seed, some fell along the path, and the birds came and ate it up. Some fell on rocky places, where it did not have much soil. It sprang up quickly, because the soil was shallow. But when the sun came up, the plants were scorched, and they withered because they had no root. Other seed fell among thorns, which grew up and choked the plants. Still other seed fell on good soil, where it produced a crop - a hundred, sixty or thirty times what was sown." Matthew 13:3-8*

The seed in the story represents the Bible, and the different conditions of the soil represent our readiness and willingness to receive God's Word. Note that not all of the seed sown by the farmer produced the result he was looking for; only the seed that was sown in the good soil. Read Matthew 13:18-23 for Jesus' explanation of the story. Cultivating "good soil" in our lives means that we allow God's Word to penetrate our thoughts and influence the motives and attitudes of our heart.

> *For the word of God is living and active. Sharper than any double-edged sword, it penetrates even to the dividing soul and spirit, joints and marrow; it judges the*

thoughts and attitudes of the heart. Hebrews
4:12

And also, our willingness to act on God's Word is central to applying it effectively:

> *Do not merely listen to the word, and so*
> *deceive yourselves. Do what it says. James*
> *1:22*

By allowing God's Word to penetrate our thoughts and shape our conscience, we can effectively examine our attitudes and motives for the decisions we make every day. When we do so, His Word becomes the most effective guide for living life.

> *But the man who looks intently into the*
> *perfect law that gives freedom (God's*
> *Word), and continues to do this, not*
> *forgetting what he has heard, but doing it -*
> *he will be blessed in what he does. James*
> *1:25*

Be encouraged to sow the seeds of the Word of God into your life; reading, understanding and applying it every day. A bountiful harvest of blessing awaits you!

Chapter Four

COMMUNICATE WITH GOD ON A PERSONAL LEVEL

INTRODUCTION: We DO have a Prayer!

The old adage, "he doesn't have a prayer" is an expression describing someone facing circumstances with impossible odds of success. Or a sportscaster may say, "He threw up a prayer," when a player makes a last-ditch attempt at scoring a three-point shot from the other end of the court as the buzzer sounds.

But God never intended our prayer life to be a last resort to overcoming difficult odds after we've exhausted all other options and resources. The truth is that God wants prayer to be the center of every Christian's life: the first place we go when in need, not the last. He wants to hear from us all day, every day, both in our times of want and need, and in times of abundance and fulfillment. Also, God wants to demonstrate His love in so many ways by being in constant communication with us as we pray.

Prayer is the key to seeing positive change in our lives and surroundings, and is foundational to growing in our walk with God.

The prayer of a righteous man is powerful and effective. James 5:16

God Wants to Hear from You

One of the many reasons prayer is viewed as a last resort when we face challenges is that we have an inaccurate perception of God. We sometimes mistakenly think that God has only a distant, impersonal level of interest in our lives. However, the fact is that God is intimately interested in your life. He created you for His pleasure, and wants to work in you and through you!

Prayer is simply defined as communication with God. Think about a close friendship you have. Sure, that person is there for you when you need them, but you talk to them all the time, don't you? You share your lives, don't you? Well, God wants to be your best friend. You can tell Him everything and anything, you can laugh with Him, you can talk about your day with Him, you can be honest with Him, you can express the desires of your heart with Him. The bottom line is He wants to hear it all! God greatly desires that you have intimate, personal communication with Him.

> *"Here I am! I stand at the door and knock. If anyone hears my voice and opens the door, I will come in and eat with him, and he with me." Revelation 3:20*

Jesus is knocking at the door of our hearts, desiring a precious time of fellowship on a personal level. Simply opening that door to Jesus' gentle request for fellowship is the beginning of a successful, effective and rewarding prayer life filled with God's blessings.

God is the true source of refuge in life, and He wants to show us His faithfulness and love - no challenge is ever too big for Him - He simply wants to hear from you.

Trust in him at all times, O people; pour out your
hearts to him, for God is our refuge. Psalm 62:8

Personal Prayer

Praying together with friends, family or even just praying before a meal are outstanding ways to communicate with God in a more public setting. But in addition to participating in corporate prayer, God wants us to participate in a personal, more private practice of prayer as well - just between you and God. Jesus has this to say about privacy in our prayers:

"But when you pray, go into your room,
close the door and pray to your Father, who
is unseen. Then your Father, who sees what
is done in secret, will reward you." Matthew
6:6

Jesus' instructions to us for praying behind closed doors indicate that God is intimately and personally interested in our lives. His desire is to enhance our personal relationship with Him through one-on-one communication. God takes notice of your commitment to have private fellowship with Him, and promises to reward and bless you.

God also wants us to be sincere and open in our communication with Him, just as we would be with a loved one. While memorizing prayers word for word is a healthy practice, the truth is that God desires an authentic expression of ourselves to Him rather than just a series of words we've memorized. Jesus has this to say about sincerity in our prayers:

36

"And when you pray, do not keep on babbling like pagans, for they think they will be heard because of their many words (empty repetitions). Do not be like them, for your Father knows what you need before you ask him." Matthew 6:7-8

While God already knows what we need and want before we ask, He still wants us to express those requests to Him with sincerity and expectation that He has our best interests in mind. He desires to answer each prayer with love and faithfulness.

Another important element of personal prayer is persistence and consistency. God never tires of hearing our requests, even if they're the same ones we've expressed to Him before. Jesus has this to say about diligence in our prayers:

"Ask and it will be given to you; seek and you will find; knock and the door will be opened to you. For everyone who asks receives; he who seeks finds; and to him who knocks, the door will be opened." Matthew 7:7-8

Setting aside a daily time for personal communication with God is important to growing in our Christian walk. Try to choose a time each day when you won't be distracted, and don't be concerned that God has his stop-watch out checking to see how much time you give Him; He doesn't. He simply wants you. **Privacy**, **sincerity** and **persistence** are three very important characteristics of your one-on-one prayer time with God and will help you build an intimate relationship Him.

You will come to enjoy this precious time, and you will come to rely on Him in a way you never have before.

God's Model for Effective Personal Prayer

The Lord's Prayer is one of the most recognized verses in the Bible. Most people have committed the Lord's Prayer to memory, or would at least recognize it upon hearing it. Jesus instructed his disciples:

> *"This then is how you should pray: 'Our Father in heaven, hallowed be your name, your kingdom come, your will be done on earth as it is in heaven. Give us today our daily bread. Forgive us our debts, as we also have forgiven our debtors. And lead us not into temptation, but deliver us from the evil one.'"*
> *Matthew 6:9-13*

The Lord's Prayer is one of the most recited prayers even to this day. But when Jesus gave these precious words to his disciples, His intentions went well beyond providing an effective prayer for us to memorize. He gave us an important framework to base all our prayers upon.

Think for a moment about what tends to limit you when you pray, and or what barriers to prayer you have. Maybe you have a tendency to focus on yourself too much. Perhaps you are easily distracted during prayer, or even tend to nod off. These are common problems all of us experience from time to time.

The Lord's Prayer provides a basis to overcome these tendencies and barriers when broken down into the components that follow.

Six Keys to a Healthy and Balanced Prayer

1. Know who you're talking to. *"Our Father in heaven..."*

When Jesus instructed His disciples to address the Father directly, the idea was likely met with some raised eyebrows. Throughout the Old Testament, only way a common person could express requests to God was through a priest. Thankfully, Jesus came to change all of that.

Because of the perfect sacrifice of Jesus on the cross to cover our sin, believers now have direct communication with the Father. That is why we pray to our Heavenly Father "in the name of Jesus." However, there are no set formulas for prayer, and praying a prayer to Jesus is just as meaningful as addressing the Father Himself. The most important part to remember is that there is now no communication barrier between God and you.

2. Reflect upon and express your adoration and thanksgiving for all He's done for you. *"...hallowed be your name..."*

By setting aside a portion of your prayer to focus specifically on praise and adoration, you remove the focus from yourself. While God wants to hear our needs and desires, He also wants us to demonstrate gratefulness for all He's done and realize it's not "all about us." In fact, it's really all about Him. He is a God of abundance and love, and praise and honor are due Him. When you reflect on the blessings God has given you and the incredible privilege it is to be in relationship with Him, you'll find it easy to express your gratitude, adoration and thanksgiving to Him. You'll also find it hard to focus on yourself.

3. Pray that God's purposes for His Church and for your life are accomplished in full. *"...your kingdom come, your will be done on earth as it is in heaven."*

Vibrant and effective prayer comes when we get our minds off of the problems of the past and onto the awesome possibilities of the future. Continually dwelling on your past will only serve to limit your future. Take on God's perspective, and don't allow previous challenges or failures to consume your thoughts and limit your thinking. Express to God your desire to achieve your full potential in Christ, and ask Him to help you enlarge your vision and dreams. He wants you to accomplish His full purpose in life, and also that of His Church.

4. Express your personal needs and wants to God, and ask Him to meet them. *"Give us today our daily bread..."*

God's love for you is profound, endless and unconditional, often compared in the Bible to a loving father's compassion for his child. He wants to hear from His child (that's you); He wants to hear about your life, your needs and desires, and He wants you to come to

Him for those needs. His love for you drives Him to bless you more that you can ever hope for.

5. Ask God to forgive you of your sins, being mindful of your need to forgive others who may have wronged you. *"Forgive us our debts, as we also have forgiven our debtors."*

Asking God to forgive us of our sins begins with first acknowledging those sins to ourselves, and then confessing them to God.

If we confess our sins, he is faithful and just and will forgive us our sins and purify us from all unrighteousness. I John 1:9

You can be assured that God has forgiven you and cleansed you of your sins. With that forgiveness, there is also freedom from guilt, shame and condemnation.

But God also asks that just as He has forgiven us, we forgive others who may have wronged us. Just as receiving forgiveness from God brings freedom, so does giving forgiveness to others - freedom from bitterness, grudges and allowing past hurts to continue hurting us.

Forgiveness, both receiving and giving it, is foundational to living a life of freedom in Christ.

6. Pray for God's guidance to help avoid temptations and situations which may not reflect well upon Him. *"...lead us not into temptation, but deliver us from the evil one."*

God has forgiven our sins and cleansed us from all unrighteousness as promised in I John 1:9, but we will still encounter temptation, living in this fallen world. This part of the Lord's Prayer emphasizes the importance of not simply resting and becoming complacent with the forgiveness God gives us, without being mindful of the importance to avoid sin in the future. While God removes the spiritual penalty of sin by forgiving us, He does not necessarily remove the harmful consequences of sin. For this reason, it is important to pray for God's help to avoid temptation.

Some Practical Considerations

On a daily basis, start giving to God whatever time you can joyfully give Him in prayer. God does not have a quota for you to meet each day. Additionally, it will be challenging at times to remain alert and avoid "nodding off." Don't be discouraged; know that you will be blessed of God as you commit your time to Him in prayer!

Chapter Five

PUT YOUR FAITH INTO ACTION

INTRODUCTION: The Golden Rule

Whether it's a politician, a business leader, a motivational speaker, or just an everyday person, people from all walks of life occasionally reference the virtues of the Golden Rule. In fact, nearly everyone has heard of it and knows its meaning.

Most people would agree that "doing unto others what we would have done to us" is a necessary part of society. In many respects, it is the fabric that holds our culture, families and friendships together. The Golden Rule demonstrates the merits of serving others, extending generosity and helping those in need.

Jesus was the author of the Golden Rule which is one of the key priorities for successful Christian living. Jesus said:

> *"So in everything, do to others what you would have them do to you, for this sums up the Law and the Prophets." Matthew 7:12*

As Christians, God calls each of us to take our faith to a level that goes beyond just believing in God. His desire is that each of us put our faith into action by touching the lives of others, thus glorifying God by showing His love and grace to them. This is truly living by the Golden Rule.

Keys to Successful Relationships

Every relationship, whether with a friend, family member, spouse, or even with God, has two fundamental components which make it successful: the love and affection shared between the individuals, and putting that love into action.

The truth is that real love is always accompanied by action; a true friend seeing another in need will respond with help. The same is true in our relationship with God. A true love for God is accompanied by action; touching God's heart by touching the lives of those around us.

Making the most of our relationships with others begins with our relationship with God. In fact, God asks that our relationships with others be an extension of our relationship with Him. Consider the two greatest commandments of the Bible as expressed by Jesus:

> *"Love the Lord your God with all your heart*
> *and with all your soul and with all your*
> *mind and with all your strength. The second*
> *is this: 'Love your neighbor as yourself '.*
> *There is no commandment greater than*
> *these." Mark 12:30-31*

As believers, our vertical relationship with God and our horizontal relationships with one another are what's most important to God - loving Him and loving others.

Growing our Love for God

Developing a love for God is perhaps a bit more challenging than with a friend or family member. One primary reason is that we cannot physically see God. So maintaining and growing a love for God requires faith.

Now faith is being sure of what we hope for and certain of what we do not see. Hebrews 11:1

Faith allows us to channel a genuine love from our hearts directly to God, even though we cannot see Him with our physical eyes. In order to grow our love for God, faith must be active in our Christian lives.

As we read God's Word, observe His love and involvement in our lives and others, and fellowship with Him in prayer, we begin to know God more and more. Knowing Him more over time nurtures a genuine maturing love for Him in our lives.

Growing that love for God out of our faith in Him also depends on demonstrating that love through action:

In the same way, faith by itself, if it is not accompanied by action, is dead. James 2:17

Our love for God through faith, accompanied by our commitment to God through action is the chemistry needed for a successful, growing relationship with Him.

While our love for God will most certainly grow as a result of putting our faith into action, it is also important to understand that these actions do not earn God's love and favor for us.

The truth is that God already loved us intimately and without condition long before we ever knew Him. God's love is the true source of ours: our love for Him and for others.

We love because he first loved us. I John 4:19

Extending Love to Others

With a vibrant and growing love for God at work in our lives, our capacity to love other people will inherently grow as well. With a maturing love for others comes a growing desire to demonstrate that love, thus fulfilling one of the most important purposes for which God created us:

For we are God's workmanship, created in Christ Jesus to do good works, which God prepared in advance for us to do. Ephesians 2:10

It has been in God's plan all along that we accompany love with action. Each one of us has a place in God's master plan to touch the lives of others through good deeds.

Each time we touch the life of another with a kind word, respond to a certain need, or just simply lend an attentive ear to a hurting heart, we not only express our love, but God's love for them through us. In this way, we become key agents to shine God's glory brightly to a world that is otherwise filled with darkness and hopelessness. Consider Jesus' words:

"You are the light of the world. A city on a hill cannot be hidden. Neither do people light a lamp and put it under a bowl. Instead they put it on its stand, and it gives light to everyone in the house. In the same way, let your light shine before men, that they may see your good deeds and praise your Father in heaven." Matthew 5:14-16

Shining our light is really allowing God's light to shine through us. There are three important ways to shine God's glory to others: being an effective witness; serving others; and fellowshipping with Christians. Putting our faith into action in these three ways enables others to experience God's love, grace and mercy, all to His glory.

Being an Effective Witness

Knowing how to be an effective witness in our everyday world begins with understanding what God wants others to observe in our lives. The short answer is of course, Jesus. But what does that mean?

Jesus provided a perfect example of how God wants us to live. While Jesus lived his earthly life in a world much different than ours' today, He embodied the full character of God and provides a relevant example for our modern world.

It is God's character that he desires to develop in our lives and to be observed by others. This is achieved only through our personal relationship with Jesus. Jesus said:

"I am the vine; you are the branches. If a man remains in me and I in him, he will bear much fruit; apart from me you can do nothing." John 15:5

"This is to my Father's glory, that you bear much fruit, showing yourselves to be my disciples." John 15:8

Just as a branch that remains in the vine it draws its life from will bear fruit, so it is for us who remain in our relationship with Jesus - we bear fruit - or demonstrate the character of God through our lives to others.

But the fruit of the Spirit is love, joy, peace, patience, kindness, goodness, faithfulness, gentleness, and selfcontrol. Against such there is no law. Galatians 5:22-23

When God's character is working in us and through us - His love, joy, peace, patience, kindness, goodness, faithfulness, gentleness and self-control we become an effective witness living out our everyday lives.

Just as it was in Jesus' day, the outward, active expression of God's character through our lives - the fruit of the Spirit - is unmistakable. It draws the attention of both Christians and unbelievers alike, and it's not uncommon for someone to inquire about it.

But in your hearts, set apart Christ as Lord. Always be prepared to give an answer to everyone who asks you to give the reason for

*the hope that you have. But do this with
gentleness and respect. 1 Peter 3:15*

Be prepared. Someone may be observing and inquire of you
when you least expect it. Your personal testimony of
salvation and of God's wonderful ongoing work in your own
life is a great starting point. Also, this book is another tool
you can use to help someone comprehend in simple terms
the wonderful message of God's love and salvation available
to all. If someone is ready to receive Christ into their life, you
can lead them in a prayer similar to the one at the conclusion
of the first chapter in this book, "The Biggest Decision in
Your Life".

Serving Others

The definition of serving is simply being available to respond
to someone's need. That response may require our time,
talent, resources and effort; but serving out of a love for God
and for others can be one of the most joyful and rewarding
experiences.

> *Each one should use whatever gift he has
> received to serve others, faithfully
> administering God's grace in its various
> forms. 1 Peter 4:10*

> *Share with God's people who are in need.
> Practice hospitality. Romans 12:13*

Responding to the needs of others can come in many forms
and can focus on the needs of Christians and unbelievers
alike. There are always opportunities to serve in the local

church either individually or as part of a team. You DO have something incredibly valuable to offer!

There are also opportunities which arise in simple one on one contact with people, or just simply observing someone's need, and responding with unsolicited assistance.

Any response you give, whether time, resources, talent or simply an encouraging word, is an act of serving. But God also understands that we have a limited capacity in what we can offer, so he expects us to show responsibility and good stewardship when making commitments.

Each man should give what he has decided
in his heart to give, not reluctantly or under
compulsion, for God loves a cheerful giver.
2 Corinthians 9:7

God's desire is for us to give of ourselves cheerfully. While at times it is difficult for some of us to say no, the truth is that overextending ourselves can ultimately rob us of the cheerfulness and joy God wants us to have when we serve.

Fellowship with Christians

Giving encouragement, love and strength to other believers is one of our greatest priorities. The fact is that we need each other. That is how God designed it. God doesn't want anyone to "go it alone."

And let us consider how we may spur one
another on toward love and good deeds. Let
us not give up meeting together as some are

50

in the habit of doing, but let us encourage one another - and all the more as you see the Day approaching. Hebrews 10:24-25

The truth is that building relationships with other Christians is crucial to our own growth. God often sets up "divine appointments" for us to minister to or encourage one another as maybe only we can.

Two are better than one, because they have a good return for their work; If one falls down, his friend can help him up. But pity the man who falls and has no one to help him up! Also, if two lie down together, they will keep warm. But how can one keep warm alone? Though one may be overpowered, two can defend themselves. A cord of three strands is not quickly broken. Ecclesiastes 4:9-12

The principle of strength in numbers applies even to Christians, and having strong relationships with fellow believers helps us grow in our walk with God!

God's plan in establishing the local church was for you to be connected to other believers. Get involved and enjoy the benefits of giving and receiving blessings from your fellow brothers and sisters in Christ!

Chapter Six

EMBRACE GOD'S HELP THROUGH LIFE'S JOURNEY

INTRODUCTION: We're Never Alone!

It is often said that life consists of a series of highs and lows, times of enjoyment and promise mixed with seasons of challenge and doubt. Life is not just a steady climb to the top; rather it is a journey that consists of hills and valleys. Everyone, believers and non-believers alike, goes through life's ups and downs.

But as Christians, we have an incredible promise from God that we never have to face the valleys in life alone. Here are His encouraging words to us:

> *Be strong and courageous. Do not be afraid or terri-*
> *fied because of them, for the Lord your God goes*
> *with you; he will never leave you nor forsake you.*
> *Deuteronomy 31:6*

The truth is that we need God's presence in both seasons of challenge and seasons of success. By knowing God is with us, we can face each challenge in life as a stepping-stone toward success rather than a decline toward despair.

No mountain is too high nor valley too low where God cannot meet us. No matter our circumstances, God is faithful, and He's always with us!

God has Come to You!

The promise of eternal life is a result of God coming to us rather than mankind trying to seek out and find God in some distant place.

Since the beginning of time, God has loved each of us with an unconditional and everlasting love. His original intention was to have a strong and vibrant relationship with each of us. However, when Adam and Eve disobeyed God in the Garden, their sin created a barrier between us and God. We became eternally separated from Him.

Rather than allowing us to remain separated from Him, God set in motion a perfect plan for restoration-one driven by His unending love and mercy for us. The goal of His plan is to fully restore even the most intimate aspects of His relationship with mankind as it existed before Adam and Eve sinned.

Over 2,000 years ago, God sent His Son to earth to remove the barrier caused by sin, and make salvation available to all.

> *"For God so loved the world that he gave his one and only Son, that whoever believes in him shall not perish but have eternal life. For God did not send his Son into the world to condemn the world, but to save the world through him." John 3:16-17*

Through his death and resurrection, Jesus made full payment on our behalf for the penalty of sin, and removed the barrier between us and God. This forgiveness is available to all who simply receive Him as their Savior.

But this was only the beginning. Before Jesus completed his time on earth to join His Father in Heaven, He described to His disciples another important element of God's broader plan to fully restore mankind to Himself:

> *"In my Father's house (Heaven) are many rooms; if it were not so, I would have told you.   I am going there to prepare a place for you.   And if I go and prepare a place for you, I will come back and take you to be with me that you also may be where I am." John 14:2-3*

Not only did God send Jesus to remove the barrier of sin, but one day in the future Jesus will return to bring all believers "home" to be with Him forever.

Heaven's Ambassador - the Holy Spirit

An ambassador is an official representative of one government sent to another to live among its people, to accomplish a mission of peace and good will. He fulfills his duties with the authority, generosity and resources of the government he represents. With utmost trust imparted to him, he accomplishes his purpose with dignity and to completion.

In many ways, the Holy Spirit's mission resembles that of an ambassador from Heaven. The Holy Spirit embodies all the authority, power and resources of God, and expresses and reveals God's love to every person on earth through His presence and His work.

As Jesus' time with His disciples was coming to a close, He told them they would not be left alone after He was gone. He told them of One who would be sent in His place to be with them, to guide them, teach them, comfort them and lead them - the Holy Spirit. Jesus said:

> *"Unless I go away, the Counselor (Holy Spirit) will not come to you; but if I go, I will send him to you."*
> *John 16:7*

After Jesus' work on earth was complete, He sent the Holy Spirit to be with us in his place until he returns again. The Holy Spirit provides guidance, leadership, comfort and counsel over our lives. Jesus described the Holy Spirit to His disciples in this way:

> *"But the Counselor, the Holy Spirit, whom the father will send in my name, will teach you all things and will remind you of everything I have said to you." John 14:26*

God's presence is with us today in the form of the Holy Spirit, and He is actively at work in our world and in our lives.

His Mission is Personal

From the beginning of creation, the Holy Spirit has been present, dwelling among us for all generations.

Now the earth was formless and empty, darkness was over the surface of the deep, and the Spirit of God was hovering over the waters. Genesis 1:2

But it was not until Jesus completed his work on the cross that the Holy Spirit's ministry became personal and intimate to every believer. Jesus told His disciples before he died that the Holy Spirit was present among them, but not yet living in them.

"The world cannot accept him (the Holy Spirit) because it neither sees him nor knows him. But you know him, for he lives with you and will be in you. I will not leave you as orphans; I will come to you." John 14:17-18

Jesus' promise of comfort to His disciples just prior to His death was that He would still be with them spiritually, through the presence of the Holy Spirit living in their lives. The work Jesus began continues in our lives through the Holy Spirit. God uses the Holy Spirit in us to do four things:

1. He makes salvation a personal reality.
2. He empowers you to live victoriously.
3. He builds Christian character to help you grow.
4. He works all things for your good.

He Makes Salvation a Personal Reality

While it was Jesus who paid for our salvation, it is God's presence through the Holy Spirit that makes salvation a personal reality to anyone who will receive it. Jesus made it clear that we don't just receive salvation when we're born. There is a spiritual rebirth that must take place, one which only the Holy Spirit can author.

> *Jesus answered, "I tell you the truth, no one can enter the kingdom of God unless he is born of water (natural birth) and the Spirit (spiritual renewal). Flesh gives birth to flesh, but the Spirit gives birth to spirit." John 3:5-6*

The moment someone receives Christ into their life, it invokes spiritual renewal in their inner person, resulting in the full removal of sin's penalty from their lives.

In addition, the Holy Spirit is at work in the lives of non-believers to reveal God's incredible love for them. Jesus said,

> *"When the Counselor (Holy Spirit) comes, whom I will send to you from the Father, the Spirit of truth who goes out from the Father, he will testify about me." John 15:26*

Today, the Holy Spirit continues this wonderful ministry of making God's love known by proclaiming Jesus, the personified love of God, and all that He represents to both believers and non-believers in our world.

He Empowers You to Live Victoriously

Without the right tools for the job, even the simplest of chores can become overwhelming. For example, removing a screw is easy with a power screwdriver, but much more tiresome and difficult without one.

One of God's top priorities is to provide us with the right tools in life. Whether it be the wisdom to face a big decision, willpower to break a bad habit, or even extra faith and trust to face an impossible situation with confidence, God is faithful to equip us with what we need to live a fulfilled and blessed life.

> *Even youths grow tired and weary, and young men stumble and fall; but those who hope in the Lord will renew their strength. They will soar on wings like eagles; they will run and not grow weary, they will walk and not be faint. Isaiah 40:30-31*

Placing our hope in Him gives us access to a limitless tool chest to equip us for whatever we face. When we are empowered from above, we live in victory!

He Builds Character to Help You Grow

Good character is not something we just receive with salvation, but is learned and developed over time. Helping us build Christ-like character is one of God's primary goals. The Holy Spirit helps us become more like Jesus by building and developing His character in us. The Bible calls this the Fruit of the Spirit.

But the fruit of the Spirit is love, joy, peace, patience, kindness, goodness, faithfulness, gentleness, and self-control. Against such there is no law. Galatians 5:22-23

In the midst of challenges, we sometimes try to overcome adversity by our own power. By doing so, we may even be tempted to compromise our Christian character to get past our difficulties, or "take a shortcut." But when we call upon the power of the Holy Spirit, He helps us stay the course with integrity, truth and honesty, no matter the circumstances.

During seasons of success, the same biblical standards should remain intact. Self-serving pride and arrogance are in direct conflict with the Christian character God wants to develop in our lives. In fact, meekness is a requirement for every Christian to continue receiving promotion from God.

"Blessed are the meek, for they will inherit the earth."
Matthew 5:5

As we face both our challenges and successes with Christ-like character, we begin to grow in our walk with God. We even begin to recognize that operating in the Fruit of the Spirit works to our ultimate good and to His honor. The more we grow in our walk with God, the more God can entrust greater blessings into our lives!

He Works All Things for Your Good

God is in control over everything in every area of our lives. He is fully able to orchestrate any circumstance to work for our benefit as believers.

> *And we know that in all things God works for the good of those who love him who have been called according to his purpose.* Romans 8:28

He is more than capable to handle even the most complicated of life's challenges, and will lead us down the course of fulfilling His plan for our lives. He simply wants us to trust Him to do so.

> *Trust in the Lord with all your heart and lean not on your own understanding; in all your ways acknowledge him, and he will make your paths straight.* Proverbs 3:5-6

Putting our trust in God does not take the place of personal responsibility and good stewardship. Rather, personal responsibility and trusting Him go hand in hand. When we do our part, God is always faithful to do His and lead us effectively.

In many cases, God's leading comes in the form of opening and closing "doors" in our circumstances. Other times, our situations require nothing short of God's divine intervention to heal, work a miracle, or accomplish something otherwise impossible to do.

Jesus looked at them and said, "With man this is
impossible, but with God all things are possible."
Matthew 19:26

Whether it may be facing an incurable disease, a financial
crisis, or even the unexpected loss of a loved one, God is
present and able to work supernaturally during these times.

God is a specialist at turning tragedy into triumph and
difficulty into joy through the Holy Spirit. Never doubt that
God is still in the "miracle-working business" today. God is
able to intervene in any impossible situation!

37205561R00037

Made in the USA
San Bernardino, CA
13 August 2016